MW00509335

INSTANT VORTEX
Air Fryer
COOKBOOK

50 QUICK AND EASY
HOME-MADE DELICIOUS RECIPES
FOR BEGINNERS

By

Jenny Ellery

© Copyright 2020, 2021 by Jenny Ellery

All rights reserved.

The following Book is reproduced below with the goal of providing information that is as accurate and reliable as possible. Regardless, purchasing this Book can be seen as consent to the fact that both the publisher and the author of this book are in no way experts on the topics discussed within and that any recommendations or suggestions that are made herein are for entertainment purposes only. Professionals should be consulted as needed prior to undertaking any of the action endorsed herein.

This declaration is deemed fair and valid by both the American Bar Association and the Committee of Publishers Association and is legally binding throughout the United States.

Furthermore, the transmission, duplication, or reproduction of any of the following work including specific information will be considered an illegal act irrespective of if it is done electronically or in print. This extends to creating a secondary or tertiary copy of the work or a recorded copy and is only allowed with the express written consent from the Publisher. All additional right reserved.

The information in the following pages is broadly considered a truthful and accurate account of facts and as such, any inattention, use, or misuse of the information in question by the reader will render any resulting actions solely under their purview. There are no scenarios in which the publisher or the original author of this work can be in any fashion deemed liable for any hardship or damages that may befall them after undertaking information described herein.

Additionally, the information in the following pages is intended only for informational purposes and should thus be thought of as universal. As befitting its nature, it is presented without assurance regarding its prolonged validity or interim quality. Trademarks that are mentioned are done without written consent and can in no way be considered an endorsement from the trademark holder.

Table of Contents

Introduction

An Air Fryer is a kitchen machine that not only occupies a prominent place in your kitchen but also in your heart.

Air Fryer cooks dishes by circulating hot air inside the appliance. It needs very little or no oil at all, thus making your diet healthy. Some models of Air Fryers like Vortex Air Fryer Oven provide you with loads of cooking options like frying, roasting, broiling, baking, reheating, dehydrating, and spit roasting.

In addition to making your food healthy, it saves you time and provides you with quick delicious food in minutes.

Air Fryers are a great substitute for traditional fryers as the latter is known to cause diabetes, heart diseases, obesity, and cancer. According to a study, people who consume fried food one to three times a week are at a 7% higher risk of heart attack and stroke compared to people who eat fried food less than once in a week.

Air fryers reduce the fat calories by 70 to 80 percent in your food, allowing you to enjoy the tasty and irresistible fried food without risking your health. You can even incorporate your crispy cravings into your diet plan through this device as you maintain your health.

Incorporate these 50 tasty and healthy recipes into your meal plan for your whole family.

Chapter 1

BREAKFAST RECIPES

Main Ingredient: **Apple**

01_Apple Fritters

UK Cuisine

Total Time:
25 minutes

Serving:
4 persons

Total Carbs:
275 g

Total Calories:
992 kcal

Ingredients:

- ¼ CUP SUGAR
- 1 EGG
- 1 AND A ½ TSP. BAKING POWDER
- 1 CUP ALL-PURPOSE FLOUR
- ¼ TSP. SALT
- ½ TSP. GROUND CINNAMON
- 2 TBSP. WHITE SUGAR
- ¼ CUP MILK
- 1 APPLE, CORED AND CHOPPED
- GLAZE:
- 1 TBSP. MILK
- ½ TSP. CARAMEL EXTRACT
- ¼ TSP. GROUND CINNAMON
- ½ CUP CONFECTIONERS' SUGAR

Method:

1. Preheat Vortex Air Fryer to 350°F.

2. Place parchment paper round in the Air Fryer.

3. Spray with non-stick cooking spray.

4. Mix together flour, egg, baking powder, 1/4 cup sugar, milk, and salt in a bowl.

5. Mix 2 tablespoons of sugar with cinnamon in a separate bowl and coat apples and then in flour mixture.

6. Air-fry for 5 minutes in the pre-heated Fryer.

7. Turnover and cook for 5 minutes more.

Main Ingredient: **Avocado**

02_Wake Up Avocado Boats

Total Time:	**Serving:**	**Total Carbs:**	**Total Calories:**
15 minutes	2 persons	95 g	1147 kcal

Ingredients:

- 2 HALVED AND PITTED AVOCADOS
- 2 SEEDED AND DICED TOMATOES
- ¼ CUP DICED RED ONION
- 2 TBSP. CHOPPED FRESH CILANTRO
- 1 TBSP. FINELY DICED JALAPENO
- 1 TBSP. LIME JUICE
- ½ TSP. SALT
- ¼ TSP. BLACK PEPPER
- 4 EGGS

Method:

1. Dice avocados and put them in a bowl.

2. Put the shell aside.

3. Mix tomatoes, onion, cilantro, jalapeno, lime juice, salt and pepper in the bowl, and refrigerate.

4. Preheat the air-fryer to air-fryer 350°F.

5. Break 1 egg in each of the shells.

6. Air Fry the shells for 5-7 minutes.

7. Top the shells with avocado salsa and serve.

Main Ingredient: **Bacon**

03_Bacon Grilled Cheese Sandwich

Total Time:
15 minutes

Serving:
2 persons

Total Carbs:
82 g

Total Calories:
1297 kcal

Ingredients:

- 4 SLICES BREAD
- 2 SLICES MILD CHEDDAR CHEESE
- 1 TBSP. BUTTER, MELTED
- 2 SLICES MOZZARELLA CHEESE
- 5-6 SLICES BACON, COOKED

Method:

1. Butter each side of the bread slices.

2. Place slices of bread with the unbuttered side up in the basket of Air Fryer.

3. Layer the remaining ingredients on the slices: cheddar cheese slice, sliced cooked bacon, mozzarella cheese slice, and buttered bread with butter side up.

4. Ingredients should be in this sequence.

5. Cook at 370°F for 4 minutes.

6. Flip the sandwiches.

7. Cook for 3 minutes more and serve.

Main Ingredient: **Biscuits**

04_Biscuit Bombs

Total Time:
25 minutes

Serving:
2 persons

Total Carbs:
59 g

Total Calories:
1187 kcal

Ingredients:

- 4 SLICES BACON, CLIPPED INTO 1/2-INCH PIECES
- 1 TBSP. BUTTER
- 2 EGGS, BEATEN
- ¼ TSP. PEPPER
- 1 CAN SOUTHERN HOME-STYLE REFRIGERATED BUTTERMILK BISCUITS
- 2 OZ. CHEDDAR CHEESE, CUT INTO TEN 3/4-INCH CUBES
- 1 EGG
- 1 TBSP. WATER

Method:

1. Cook bacon over medium-high heat in a skillet until crisp and remove.
2. Cook 2 beaten eggs and pepper in butter in a skillet until thickened.
3. Remove eggs and add bacon.
4. Cut dough into 5 biscuits.
5. Separate each biscuit into 2 layers.
6. Press each into 4-inch round.
7. Put 1 tablespoon egg mixture in the center of each round.
8. Top with one piece of the cheese.
9. Fold dough and seal.
10. Brush biscuits with egg wash prepared by remaining eggs and water.
11. Cut two 8-inch rounds of parchment paper...

12. Place an 8-inch round parchment paper in the bottom of the Air Fryer basket.

13. Spray with cooking spray.

14. Place 5 of the biscuit bombs on paper.

15. Spray both sides of a second parchment round with cooking spray.

16. Top biscuit bombs in the basket with a second parchment round, then top with remaining 5 biscuit bombs.

17. Cook biscuits at 325°F for 8 minutes.

18. Turn biscuits.

19. Cook 4 to 6 minutes and serve.

Main Ingredient: **Bread**

05_French Toast Sticks

Total Time:	**Serving:**	**Total Carbs:**	**Total Calories:**
15 minutes	2 persons	111 g	767 kcal

Ingredients:

- 2 EGGS
- 4 PIECES OF BREAD
- ¼ TSP. SALT
- ¼ TSP. GROUND CLOVE
- ¼ TSP. NUTMEG
- ¼ TSP. CINNAMON SEEDS
- 2 TBSP. BUTTER

Method:

1. Pre-heat Air Fryer to 356°F.

2. Beat two eggs with eggs, cinnamon, nutmeg, ground cloves, and salt in a bowl.

3. Butter bread slices and cut into strips.

4. Coat strips with egg mixture and arrange in the Air Fryer.

5. After 2 minutes of cooking spray bread with cooking spray and flip.

6. Now cook for 4 more minutes.

7. Top with icing sugar and serve.

Main Ingredient: **Cranberry**

06_Gluten-Free Cranberry Pecan Muffins

Total Time:	**Serving:**	**Total Carbs:**	**Total Calories:**
25 minutes	3-4 persons	131 g	573kcal

Ingredients:

- 1/4 CUP CASHEW MILK
- 2 LARGE EGGS
- 1/2 TSP. VANILLA EXTRACT
- 1 1/2 CUPS ALMOND FLOUR
- 1/4 CUP MONK FRUIT
- 1 TSP. BAKING POWDER
- 1/4 TSP. CINNAMON
- 1/8 TSP. SALT
- 1/2 CUP FRESH CRANBERRIES
- 1/4 CUP CHOPPED PECANS

Method:

1. Blend milk, eggs, vanilla extract, almond flour, sugar, baking powder, cinnamon, and salt.

2. Add 1/2 of the fresh cranberries and the pecans.

3. Add the mixture to silicone muffin cups.

4. Top each of the muffins with remaining fresh cranberries.

5. Cook muffins in the Air Fryer basket at 325° F for 12-15 minutes.

6. Drizzle with a maple glaze if desired and serve.

Main Ingredient: **Egg**

07_Breakfast Frittata

Italian Cuisine

Total Time:
30 minutes

Serving:
2 persons

Total Carbs:
32 g

Total Calories:
1109 kcal

Ingredients:

- ¼ POUND BREAKFAST SAUSAGE FULLY COOKED AND CRUMBLED

- 4 EGGS, BEATEN

- ½ CUP SHREDDED CHEDDAR-MONTEREY JACK CHEESE BLEND

- 2 TBSP. RED BELL PEPPER, DICED

- 1 GREEN ONION, CHOPPED

- ¼ TSP. CAYENNE PEPPER

Method:

1. Mix sausage, eggs, Cheddar-Monterey Jack cheese, bell pepper, onion, and cayenne in a bowl and mix to combine.

2. Preheat the Air Fryer to 360 °F.

3. Spray a non-stick 6x2-inch cake pan with cooking spray.

4. Put the egg mixture in the cake pan.

5. Cook pan in the Air Fryer for 18 to 20 minutes.

Main Ingredient: **Egg**

08_Cheese Omelette

Ancient Persian Cuisine

Total Time: 8 minutes	**Serving:** 1-2 persons	**Total Carbs:** 16 g	**Total Calories:** 477 kcal

Ingredients:

- 1/4 CUP MILK
- 2 EGGS
- ¼ TSP. SALT
- ¼ CUP HAM
- ¼ CUP DICED BELL PEPPERS
- 1 TSP. GARDEN HERB MCCORMICK GOOD MORNING BREAKFAST SEASONING
- ¼ CUP MUSHROOMS
- 1/4 CUP CHEESE, SHREDDED

Method:

1. Mix eggs and milk well.
2. Add salt and vegetables to the mixture.
3. Put the egg mixture in a greased 6"x3" pan.
4. Cook at the eggs for 8-10 minutes at 350°F.
5. Midway cooking sprinkle the breakfast seasoning on the eggs and add the cheese on the top.
6. Top with extra green onions if desired and serve.

Main Ingredient: **Egg**

09_Egg Rolls

Total Time:
25 minutes

Serving:
3 persons

Total Carbs:
125 g

Total Calories:
1404 kcal

Ingredients:

- 2 EGGS
- 2 TBSP. MILK
- ¼ TBSP. SALT
- ¼ TBSP. PEPPER
- 1/2 CUP SHREDDED CHEDDAR CHEESE
- 2 SAUSAGE PATTIES
- 6 EGG ROLL WRAPPERS
- 1 TBSP. OLIVE OIL

Method:

1. Cook sausage in a skillet and chop.
2. Whisk eggs, milk, a pinch of both salt and pepper.
3. Make scrambled eggs.
4. Add sausage.
5. Put 1 tbsp. cheese on the bottom third of the wrapper.
6. Top with egg mixture.
7. Brush all edges of egg roll wrapper and seal.
8. Spray rolls with cooking spray.
9. Set to 400°F for 11 minutes.
10. After 5 minutes, turn egg rolls
11. Cook for another 3 minutes and serve.

Main Ingredient: **Egg**

10_Hard Boiled Eggs

Roman Cuisine

Total Time:
20 minutes

Serving:
3 persons

Total Carbs:
4 g

Total Calories:
328 kcal

Ingredients:

- 6 LARGE EGGS

Method:

1. Place eggs in the Air Fryer basket.

2. Air Fryer for 16 minutes at 500°F.

3. Place eggs in a bowl with ice and cold water.

4. Let cool for 5 minutes.

5. Peel and serve.

Main Ingredient: **Ham**

11_ Ham and Egg Toast Cups

Total Time:
20 minutes

Serving:
2 persons

Total Carbs:
161 g

Total Calories:
1170 kcal

Ingredients:

- 4 EGGS
- 8 SLICES OF TOAST
- 2 SLICES OF HAM
- ½ TBSP. BUTTER
- ¼ TSP. SALT
- ¼ TSP. PEPPER
- ¼ CUPS CHEESE

Method:

1. Brush ramekins with butter.

2. Flatten 8 slices of toast.

3. Put a slice of flattened toast in each ramekin.

4. Place another slice of toast on top.

5. Cut 2 slices of ham into 8 strips.

6. Line 2 strips of ham in each ramekin.

7. Crack an egg into each toast cup.

8. Add salt and pepper and cheese.

9. Put ramekins into the Air fryer for 15 minutes at 320°F and serve.

Main Ingredient: **Peanut Butter**

12_Peanut Butter
and Jelly Air Fried Doughnuts

Total Time:	**Serving:**	**Total Carbs:**	**Total Calories:**
25 minutes	2-3 persons	352 g	1092 kcal

Ingredients:

- 1 AND A 1/4 CUPS ALL-PURPOSE FLOUR
- 1/3 CUP SUGAR
- 1/2 TSP. BAKING POWDER
- 1/2 TSP. BAKING SODA
- 3/4 TSP. SALT
- 1 EGG
- 1/2 CUP BUTTERMILK
- 1 TSP. VANILLA
- 2 TBSP. UNSALTED BUTTER, MELTED AND COOLED
- 1 TBSP. MELTED BUTTER FOR BRUSHING THE TOPS
- 1/2 CUP BLUEBERRY JELLY
- GLAZE:
- 1/2 CUP POWDERED SUGAR
- 2 TBSP. MILK
- 2 TBSP. PEANUT BUTTER
- ¼ TSP. SALT

Method:

1. Combine flour, baking powder, sugar, baking soda, and salt.

2. Whisk egg, melted butter, buttermilk, and vanilla in a separate bowl.

3. Make a dough of all the above ingredients and kneed.

4. Flat-it out to a 3/4" thickness.

5. Cut out dough rounds and brush with melted butter.

6. Cut out 2" pieces of parchment paper and place each dough round on the paper, then into the Air Fryer.

7. Fry at 350°F for 11 minutes.

8. Fill doughnuts with jelly.

9. Whisk together the glaze ingredients and serve with glaze.

Main Ingredient: **Potatoes**

13_Breakfast Potatoes

Total Time:
30 minutes

Serving:
2 persons

Total Carbs:
180 g

Total Calories:
501 kcal

Ingredients:

- 1 AND A 1/2 POUND POTATOES, DICED
- 1/4 ONION, CHOPPED
- 1 GREEN BELL PEPPER, CHOPPED
- 2 GARLIC CLOVES, MINCED
- 1 TBSP. OLIVE OIL
- 1/4 TSP. PEPPER
- 1/2 TSP. SALT
- 1/2 TSP. PAPRIKA

Method:

1. Dice potatoes and soak in cold water for 30 minutes.

2. Chop onion, bell pepper, and potatoes.

3. Mince garlic.

4. Mix all the ingredients in a bowl.

5. Cook in the Air Fryer at 390-400°F for 10 minutes.

6. Shake the basket and cook 10 minutes more.

7. Shake the basket again and cook for 5 minutes more and serve.

Main Ingredient: **Puff Pastry**

14_Toad in the Hole Tarts

UK Cuisine

Total Time:
30 minutes

Serving:
4 persons

Total Carbs:
134 g

Total Calories:
2120 kcal

Ingredients:

- 1 SHEET FROZEN PUFF PASTRY, THAWED
- 4 TBSP. SHREDDED CHEDDAR CHEESE
- 4 TBSP. DICED COOKED HAM
- 4 EGGS
- ¼ CUP CHOPPED FRESH CHIVES

Method:

1. Preheat the Air Fryer to 400 °F.
2. Cut pastry sheets into 4 squares.
3. Put 2 pastry squares in the Air Fryer basket and cook 6 to 8 minutes.
4. Use a spoon to press each square gently in the middle.
5. Put 1 tablespoon of cheddar cheese and 1 tablespoon ham in each hole and pour 1 egg on top of each.
6. Return basket to the Air Fryer.
7. Cook for 6 minutes more.
8. Garnish tarts with chives.

Main Ingredient: **Sausage**

15_ Breakfast Sausage

USA Cuisine

Total Time: 20 minutes	**Serving:** 8 persons	**Total Carbs:** 39 g	**Total Calories:** 2116 kcal

Ingredients:

- 1 LB. GROUND PORK
- 1 LB. GROUND TURKEY
- 2 TSP. FENNEL SEEDS
- 2 TSP. DRY RUBBED SAGE
- 2 TSP. GARLIC POWDER
- 1 TSP. PAPRIKA
- 1 TSP. SEA SALT
- 1 TSP. DRIED THYME
- 1 TBSP. REAL MAPLE SYRUP

Method:

1. Mix pork and turkey in a large bowl.
2. Mix remaining ingredients: fennel, sage, garlic powder, paprika, salt, and thyme in a separate bowl.
3. Mix spices with meat.
4. Spoon into small balls and flatten into patties.
5. Put balls in batches at 370°F for 10 minutes.
6. Remove and serve.

Chapter 2

LUNCH RECIPES

Main Ingredient: **Avocado**

16_Avocado Fries

Total Time:
15 minutes

Serving:
1-2 persons

Total Carbs:
152 g

Total Calories:
1188 kcal

Ingredients:

- 1/2 CUP ALL-PURPOSE FLOUR
- 1 AND A 1/2 TSP. BLACK PEPPER
- 2 LARGE EGGS
- 1 TBSP. WATER
- 1/2 CUP PANKO BREADCRUMBS
- 2 AVOCADOS, CUT INTO 8 WEDGES EACH
- 1/4 TSP. KOSHER SALT
- 1/4 CUP NO-SALT KETCHUP
- 2 TBSP. CANOLA MAYONNAISE
- 1 TBSP. APPLE CIDER VINEGAR
- 1 TBSP. SRIRACHA CHILI SAUCE

Method:

1. Combine flour and pepper in a dish.

2. Whisk eggs with water in a second dish.

3. Put the panko in a third shallow dish.

4. Gently dip avocado wedges in flour and then in the egg mixture.

5. Coat wedges with panko and then with cooking spray.

6. Cook wedges at 400°F until golden for 7 to 8 minutes and turn avocado wedges over halfway through cooking.

7. Remove from Air Fryer and sprinkle with salt.

8. Whisk ketchup, mayonnaise, vinegar, and Sriracha in a small bowl.

9. Serve avocado fries with the sauce.

Main Ingredient: **Avocado**

17_Bacon Avocado Fries

Total Time:
15 minutes

Serving:
3-4 persons

Total Carbs:
112 g

Total Calories:
1590 kcal

Ingredients:

- 3 AVOCADOS

- 24 THIN STRIPS OF BACON

- 1/4 CUP. RANCH DRESSING

Method:

1. Preheat oven to 425°F.

2. Slice each avocado into 8 equally-sized wedges.

3. Wrap each wedge in bacon.

4. Bake bacon for 12 to 15 minutes.

5. Serve with ranch dressing.

Main Ingredient: **Banana**

18_Banana Bread

USA Cuisine

Total Time:
45 minutes

Serving:
4-5 persons

Total Carbs:
266 g

Total Calories:
989 kcal

Ingredients:

- 3/4 CUP WHITE WHOLE WHEAT FLOUR
- 1 TSP. CINNAMON
- 1/2 TSP. KOSHER SALT
- 1/4 TSP. BAKING SODA
- 2 MEDIUM RIPE BANANAS
- 2 LARGE MASHED EGGS,
- 1/2 CUP GRANULATED SUGAR
- 1/3 CUP PLAIN NONFAT YOGURT
- 2 TBSP. VEGETABLE OIL
- 1 TSP. VANILLA EXTRACT
- 2 TSP. TOASTED ROUGHLY CHOPPED WALNUTS

Method:

1. Put parchment paper in a 6-inch round cake pan and coat with cooking spray.

2. Mix flour, cinnamon, salt, and baking soda in a medium bowl.

3. In a separate medium bowl, mix mashed bananas, eggs, sugar, yogurt, oil, and vanilla.

4. Pour batter into prepared pan and sprinkle with walnuts.

5. Set the Air Fryer to 310°F and then place the pan in the Air Fryer.

6. Cook until a wooden pick inserted in the middle comes out clean, 30 to 35 minutes, turning pan halfway through cook time.

7. Let it cool and serve.

Main Ingredient: **Bread**

19_Italian Bread Salad with Olives

Total Time:
25 minutes

Serving:
4 persons

Total Carbs:
191 g

Total Calories:
1215 kcal

Ingredients:

- 5 CUPS CUBED CIABATTA BREAD
- 1/3 CUP OLIVE OIL
- 1 GARLIC CLOVE, MINCED
- 1/8 TSP. PEPPER
- 2 TBSP. BALSAMIC VINEGAR
- 1/8 TSP. SALT
- 1 TOMATO, CHOPPED
- 2 TBSP. SLICED RIPE OLIVES
- 2 TBSP. CHOPPED FRESH BASIL
- 1 TBSP. CHOPPED FRESH ITALIAN PARSLEY
- 2 TBSP. SHREDDED PARMESAN CHEESE

Method:

1. Preheat Air Fryer to 350°F.
2. Put bread cubes in a bowl.
3. In another bowl, mix oil, garlic, and pepper; drizzle 2 tablespoons over bread.
4. Cook bread until crisp and light brown, 7-9 minutes.
5. Combine vinegar, salt and tomatoes, olives, and herbs into reserved oil mixture.
6. Add bread to the tomato mixture.
7. Sprinkle with cheese and serve.

Main Ingredient: **Cauliflower**

20_Cauliflower Chickpea Tacos

Total Time:
30 minutes

Serving:
4 persons

Total Carbs:
725 g

Total Calories:
3022 kcal

Ingredients:

- 19 OZ. CAN OF CHICKPEAS
- 4 CUPS CAULIFLOWER FLORETS CUT INTO BITE-SIZED PIECES
- 2 TBSP. OLIVE OIL
- 8 SMALL TORTILLAS
- 2 TBSP. TACO SEASONING
- 2 AVOCADOS, SLICED
- 6 TBSP. COCONUT YOGURT
- 4 CUPS CABBAGE, SHREDDED

Method:

1. Pre-heat Vortex Air Fryer to 390°F.

2. Mix cauliflower and chickpeas with taco seasoning and olive oil.

3. Cook in the Air Fryer, shaking the basket midway, for 20 minutes.

4. Serve tacos with avocado slices, cabbage, and coconut yogurt.

Main Ingredient: **Chicken**

21_Caribbean Spiced Chicken

Total Time:
20 minutes

Serving:
8 persons

Total Carbs:
257 g

Total Calories:
2250 kcal

Ingredients:

- 3 LB. BONELESS, SKINLESS CHICKEN THIGH FILLETS
- ¼ TSP. BLACK PEPPER
- ¼ TSP. SALT
- 1 TBSP. GROUND CORIANDER SEED
- 1 TBSP. GROUND CINNAMON
- 1 TBSP. CAYENNE PEPPER
- 1 AND A 1/2 TSP. GROUND GINGER
- 1 AND 1/2 TSP. GROUND NUTMEG
- 3 TBSP. COCONUT OIL, MELTED

Method:

1. Coat chicken with salt and pepper.

2. Combine coriander, cinnamon, cayenne, ginger, and nutmeg.

3. Coat chicken with spices and olive oil.

4. Air Fry chicken in batches at 390°F for 10 minutes.

Main Ingredient: **Chickpeas**

22_Roast Vegetable Salad
with Crunchy Fried Chickpeas

Total Time:
25 minutes

Serving:
6 persons

Total Carbs:
935 g

Total Calories:
2931 kcal

Ingredients:

- 1 MEDIUM SWEET POTATO
- 1/4 CUP RED CAPSICUM
- 1/4 CUP YELLOW CAPSICUM
- 1 RED ONION
- 4 SMALL CHAT POTATOES
- 250G CHERRY TOMATOES
- 300G BAG OF MIXED SALAD LEAVES
- JUICE OF 2 LEMONS
- 2 TBSP. CHOPPED CAPERS
- 1 TSP. OF CUMIN
- A BUNCH OF FRESH PARSLEY
- 1 AVOCADO
- 1 TBSP. OLIVE OIL
- ¼ TSP. SALT
- ¼ TSP. PEPPER
- 1 TIN OF CHICKPEAS
- 1 TSP. MUSTARD POWDER

Method:

1. Chop all the vegetables and season with salt, pepper.

2. Cook for 25 minutes at 392°F and shake the basket midway through.

3. Refrigerate.

4. Mash avocados with oil, lemon juice, chopped parsley, capers, and cumin.

5. Mix with salad and serve.

Main Ingredient: **Egg**

23_German Pancakes

German Cuisine

Total Time:	**Serving:**	**Total Carbs:**	**Total Calories:**
13 minutes	2-3 persons	224 g	930 kcal

Ingredients:

- 3 EGGS
- 1 CUP WHOLE WHEAT FLOUR
- 1 CUP ALMOND MILK
- ¼ TSP. SALT
- 2 TBSP. UNSWEETENED APPLESAUCE

Method:

1. Mix all ingredients for the batter to a blender and blend until smooth.

2. If the batter is thick, add tablespoons of milk or applesauce.

3. Pour batter in a cooking sprayed ramekin.

4. Air Fry for 6 to 8 minutes at 390°F and serve.

Main Ingredient: **Jalapeno**

24_Jalapeno Poppers

Mexican Cuisine

Total Time:
18 minutes

Serving:
4 persons

Total Carbs:
114 g

Total Calories:
924 kcal

Ingredients:

- 10 JALAPENO PEPPERS HALVED AND DE-SEEDED

- 8 OZ. OF CREAM CHEESE

- 1/4 CUP FRESH PARSLEY

- 3/4 CUP GLUTEN-FREE TORTILLA OR BREAD CRUMBS

Method:

1. Mix 1/2 of crumbs, parsley, and cream cheese.

2. Stuff peppers with this mixture.

3. Press the pepper tops into the remaining 1/4 cup of crumbs.

4. Cook in an Air Fryer at 370°F for 6-8 minutes and serve.

Main Ingredient: **Lettuce**

25_Chicken Caesar Salad
with Garlic Parmesan Croutons
Mexican Cuisine

Total Time:
17 minutes

Serving:
4 persons

Total Carbs:
145 g

Total Calories:
2574 kcal

Ingredients:

- 2 TBSP. OLIVE OIL
- 2 TBSP. LEMON JUICE
- 2 TBSP. HONEY
- 2 TBSP. WORCESTERSHIRE SAUCE
- ½ TSP. DRIED THYME
- 1 TSP. SALT
- ½ TSP. DRIED OREGANO
- ¼ TSP. GROUND BLACK PEPPER
- 3 HEARTS ROMAINE LETTUCE
- 12 OZ. CHICKEN BREASTS
- ¼ CUP PARMIGIANO-REGGIANO CHEESE, SHAVED
- DRESSING:
- 2 EGG YOLKS
- ¼ TSP. SALT ....

Method:

1. Combine olive oil, lemon juice, thyme, oregano, salt, Worcestershire sauce, honey and black pepper in a bowl.

2. Put chicken breasts in a plastic zip bag and add the above mixture. Refrigerate overnight.

3. Whisking egg yolks, pepper, anchovy paste, lemon juice, salt and garlic.

4. Whisk in oils slowly.

5. Coat bread cubes with Italian seasoning, salt, olive oil, black pepper, and Parmesan cheese.

6. Air Fry for 5 minutes at 380°F.

7. Air Fry chicken for 12 minutes at 380°F, flipping it midway.

8. Put the romaine lettuce in a bowl.

9. Season with Caesar dressing, black pepper, cheese, and

- JUICE FROM ½ LEMON
- ¼ TSP. BLACK PEPPER
- ½ CLOVE GARLIC
- 1 TSP. ANCHOVY PASTE
- ¼ CUP OLIVE OIL
- ½ CUP CANOLA OIL
- CROUTONS:
- 4 SLICES ITALIAN BREAD, CUBED
- 1 TSP. ITALIAN SEASONING
- 1 TBSP. OLIVE OIL
- 2 TBSP. GRATED PARMESAN CHEESE
- ¼ TSP. BLACK PEPPER
- ¼ TSP. SALT

croutons.

10. Serve with chicken slices.

Main Ingredient: **Mozzarella**

26_Tandoori Paneer Naan Pizza

Total Time:
20 minutes

Serving:
2 persons

Total Carbs:
144 g

Total Calories:
975 kcal

Ingredients:

- 2 GARLIC NAAN
- 1/4 CUP GRAPE TOMATOES, HALVED
- 1/4 CUP PIZZA SAUCE
- 1/4 CUP RED ONIONS, SLICED
- 3/4 CUP MOZZARELLA, GRATED
- 1/4 CUP BELL PEPPER, SLICED
- 2 TBSP. CILANTRO, CHOPPED
- 2 TBSP. FETA
- TANDOORI PANEER:
- 1/2 CUP PANEER SMALL CUBES
- 1/2 TSP. GARAM MASALA
- 1 TBSP. YOGURT THICK
- 1/2 TSP. GARLIC POWDER
- 1/2 TSP. KASHMIRI RED CHILI POWDER
- 1/4 TSP. GROUND TURMERIC
- 1/4 TSP SALT

Method:

1. Mix all the ingredients in a bowl for Tandoori Paneer.

2. Add sauce on each naan.

3. Spread mozzarella cheese on the naans.

4. Put the paneer cubes which are mixed with spices and yogurt on naans.

5. Top with bell peppers, red onions, and grape tomatoes.

6. Top mozzarella on the veggies.

7. Sprinkle feta cheese on top.

8. Add some chopped cilantro.

9. Cook on for 8-10 minutes 350°F.

10. Top with chili flakes and serve.

Main Ingredient: **Pickles**

27_Low Carb Pickles

Indian Cuisine

Total Time:	**Serving:**	**Total Carbs:**	**Total Calories:**
40 minutes	7 persons	26 g	580 kcal

Ingredients:

- 1 EGG
- 1/4 TSP. CAYENNE PEPPER
- 3/4 CUP HEAVY CREAM
- 1/2 CUP ALMOND FLOUR
- 2 OZ. PORK RINDS
- 2 TSP. PAPRIKA
- 2 TBSP. FREEZE-DRIED DILL
- 35 DILL PICKLE SLICES
- 2 TSP. BLACK PEPPER

Method:

1. Mix together egg, heavy cream, and cayenne.

2. Put 1/2 cup crumbled pork rinds in a shallow bowl.

3. In another bowl, mix the rest of the pork rinds with dill, paprika, almond flour, and black pepper.

4. Coat pickle slices with plain pork rinds.

5. Coat pickles with egg wash.

6. Coat pickles with almond flour mixture.

7. Air Fry pickles at 390°F and serve with Ranch dressing and Sriracha Mayo.

Main Ingredient: **Potatoes**

28_Loaded Potatoes

Peruvian Cuisine

Total Time: 25 minutes	**Serving:** 1-2 persons	**Total Carbs:** 119 g	**Total Calories:** 536 kcal

Ingredients:

- 11-OUNCE BABY YUKON GOLD POTATOES
- 1 TSP. OLIVE OIL
- 2 CENTER-CUT BACON SLICES
- 1 AND A 1/2 TBSP. CHOPPED FRESH CHIVES
- 1/2 OUNCE FINELY SHREDDED REDUCED-FAT CHEDDAR CHEESE
- 2 TBSP. REDUCED-FAT SOUR CREAM
- 1/8 TSP. KOSHER SALT

Method:

1. Brush potatoes with oil.

2. Cook potatoes at 350°F for 25 minutes, stirring potatoes occasionally.

3. Meanwhile, cook bacon in a medium skillet over medium until crispy for about 7 minutes.

4. Remove bacon from pan and crumble.

5. Top potatoes with chives, cheese, sour cream, salt, and crumbled bacon.

Main Ingredient: **Sweet Potatoes**

29_Sweet Potato Toast

Total Time:	**Serving:**	**Total Carbs:**	**Total Calories:**
35 minutes	1-2 persons	246 g	467 kcal

Ingredients:

- 1 SWEET POTATO
- 1 TBSP. PRIMAL PALATE MEAT AND POTATOES BLEND
- PRIMAL KITCHEN FOODS AVOCADO OIL SPRAY

Method:

1. Reheat the Air Fryer to 375 - 390°F.

2. Slice sweet potato lengthwise into 1/3-inch thick pieces.

3. Spray with avocado oil spray.

4. Season with Primal Palate Meat and Potatoes blend

5. Air Fry for 15 minutes, turn, and Air Fry for an additional 15 minutes.

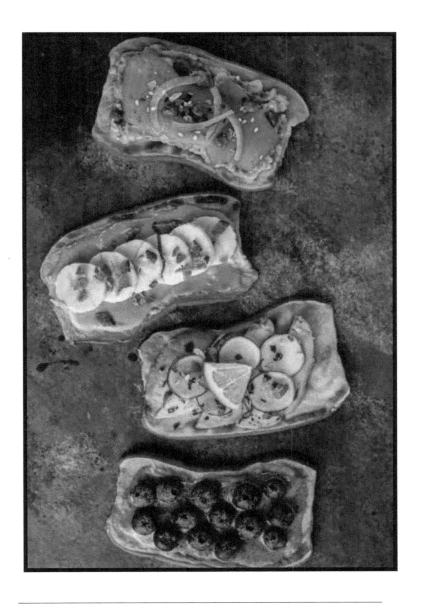

Main Ingredient: **Tortilla**

30_Corn Tortilla Chips
Mexican Cuisine

Total Time:
5 minutes

Serving:
2 persons

Total Carbs:
744 g

Total Calories:
3430 kcal

Ingredients:

- 8 CORN TORTILLAS
- 1 TBSP. OLIVE OIL
- ¼ TBSP. SALT

Method:

1. Preheat Air Fryer to 392°F.
2. Cut corn tortillas into triangles.
3. Brush with olive oil and cook for 3 minutes.
4. Sprinkle with salt and serve.

Chapter 3

DINNER RECIPES

Main Ingredient: **Artichoke**

31_Artichoke Crostini
with Hummus and Cashews

Total Time:
20 minutes

Serving:
10 persons

Total Carbs:
189 g

Total Calories:
1961 kcal

Ingredients:

- FOR CASHEWS
- 1/2 CUP RAW CASHEW PIECES
- 1 TBSP. LEMON JUICE
- 1 TBSP. EXTRA VIRGIN OLIVE OIL
- 1 TSP. BALSAMIC VINEGAR
- 1/2 TSP. DRIED OREGANO
- 1/2 TSP. DRIED BASIL
- 1/8 TSP. GRANULATED ONION
- 1/4 TSP. SALT
- 1 CLOVE GARLIC ZESTED
- FOR CROSTINI
- 1 CUP GRILLED ARTICHOKE HEARTS, SLICED
- 1 BAGUETTE CUT INTO 1/2 INCH SLICES
- 1 AND 1/2 CUPS HUMMUS
- 1 TBSP. EXTRA VIRGIN OLIVE OIL

Method:

1. Mix raw cashew pieces with lemon juice vinegar, extra virgin olive oil, dried basil, dried oregano, zested garlic, granulated onion and a pinch of salt.

2. Air Fry baguette slices at 380°F for 3 to 4 minutes, turning midway cooking.

3. Top crostini with hummus and cashews.

4. Put a sliver of grilled artichoke heart onto each crostini.

5. Serve on a platter.

Main Ingredient: **Beef**

32_Empanadas

Spanish and Portugal Cuisine

Total Time:	**Serving:**	**Total Carbs:**	**Total Calories:**
20-30 minutes	4 persons	243 g	1515 kcal

Ingredients:

- 1 TBSP. OLIVE OIL
- 1/4 CUP FINELY CHOPPED WHITE ONION
- 3-OZ. LEAN GROUND BEEF
- 3 OUNCES FINELY CHOPPED CREMINI MUSHROOMS
- 6 PITTED AND CHOPPED GREEN OLIVES
- 2 TSP. FINELY CHOPPED GARLIC
- 1/4 TSP. PAPRIKA
- 1/8 TSP. GROUND CINNAMON
- 1/4 TSP. GROUND CUMIN
- 8 SQUARE GYOZA WRAPPERS
- 1/2 CUP CHOPPED TOMATOES
- 1 LARGE EGG

Method:

1. Cook beef in a skillet for 3 minutes at low heat.

2. Add mushrooms and cook for 6 minutes.

3. Add garlic, paprika, cumin, olives, and cinnamon.

4. Cook mixture until mushrooms are tender.

5. Put tomatoes in and stir occasionally.

6. Place about 1.5 tablespoons stuffing in the center of each gyoza wrapper.

7. Brush edges of gyoza wrappers with egg, fold wrappers over and seal edges.

8. Repeat process with remaining wrappers.

9. Cook empanadas in batches in a single layer in the Air Fryer basket, and cook for 7 minutes at 400°F and serve.

Main Ingredient: **Beef**

33_Meatloaf

Belgium, German and Scandinavian Cuisine

| **Total Time:** 45 minutes | **Serving:** 4 persons | **Total Carbs:** 44 g | **Total Calories:** 1338 kcal |

Ingredients:

- 1-POUND LEAN GROUND BEEF
- 1 EGG
- 3 TBSP. DRY BREAD CRUMBS
- 1 SMALL ONION, CHOPPED
- 1 TBSP. CHOPPED THYME
- 1 TSP. SALT
- ¼ TSP. BLACK PEPPER
- 2 MUSHROOMS, SLICED
- 1 TBSP. OLIVE OIL

Method:

1. Stir together ground beef, egg, onion, thyme, salt, bread crumbs, and pepper in a bowl.

2. Transfer beef mixture to a baking pan.

3. Add mushrooms to the top and coat with olive oil.

4. Air Fry beef at 392°F for 25 minutes and serve.

Main Ingredient: **Cheese**

34_Cheeseburgers

USA Cuisine

Total Time:	**Serving:**	**Total Carbs:**	**Total Calories:**
30 minutes	2 persons	143 g	1811 kcal

Ingredients:

- 1 SLICE WHITE SANDWICH BREAD
- 1 AND A 1/2 TBSP. LOW-FAT MILK
- 1/2 TSP. GARLIC POWDER
- 1/2 TSP. SALT
- 1/4 TSP. GROUND BLACK PEPPER
- 1-POUND GROUND BEEF
- 2 SLICES CHEDDAR CHEESE
- 2 BRIOCHE BUNS, HALVED

Method:

1. Mix bread pieces with milk, ground beef, garlic powder, salt, and pepper in a bowl until well incorporated.

2. Shape mixture into 2 equal patties.

3. Push from the center.

4. Cook for 8 to 10 minutes at 350°F.

5. Flip and cook for 8 to 10 minutes.

6. Top patties with cheese and cook for 20 to 30 seconds.

7. Place on buns and serve.

Main Ingredient: **Chicken**

35_Chicken Breast

Total Time:
20 minutes

Serving:
4 persons

Total Carbs:
10 g

Total Calories:
693 kcal

Ingredients:

- 1 LB. BONELESS SKINLESS CHICKEN BREASTS
- 1 TBSP. OLIVE OIL
- 1/4 CUP BREAD CRUMBS
- 1/2 TSP. SALT
- 1/4 TSP. BLACK PEPPER
- 1/2 TSP. PAPRIKA
- 1/8 TSP. GARLIC POWDER
- 1/8 TSP. ONION POWDER
- 1/16 TSP. CAYENNE PEPPER

Method:

1. Heat Air Fryer to 390°F.
2. Slice chicken breasts in half horizontally.
3. Brush each side lightly with olive oil.
4. Coat chicken with breading ingredients.
5. Cook for 4 minutes, turn, then two more minutes and serve.

Main Ingredient: **Chicken**

36_Garlic Rosemary Rotisserie Chicken

Total Time:	**Serving:**	**Total Carbs:**	**Total Calories:**
1 hour	6 persons	427 g	3753 kcal

Ingredients:

- 3-4 LB. WHOLE CHICKEN
- 1/4 CUP AVOCADO OIL
- 3 CLOVES GARLIC, MINCED
- 1 TSP. DRIED ROSEMARY
- 1 TSP. SALT
- 1 TSP. PEPPER

Method:

1. Coat chicken with half of salt and pepper, oil, garlic, and rosemary.

2. Air Fry chicken at 350°F for 30 minutes.

3. Turn the chicken over and coat with the remaining oil mixture.

4. Air Fry for another 30 minutes and serve.

Main Ingredient: **Chicken**

37_Mexican-Style Stuffed Chicken Breasts

Mexican Cuisine

Total Time:
30 minutes

Serving:
2 persons

Total Carbs:
29 g

Total Calories:
476 kcal

Ingredients:

- 4 TSP. CHILI POWDER, DIVIDED
- 4 TSP. GROUND CUMIN, DIVIDED
- 1 SKINLESS, BONELESS CHICKEN BREAST
- 2 TSP. CHIPOTLE FLAKES
- 2 TSP. MEXICAN OREGANO
- ¼ TSP. SALT
- ¼ TSP PEPPER
- ½ RED BELL PEPPER, SLICED
- ½ ONION, SLICED
- 1 JALAPENO PEPPER, SLICED
- 2 TSP. CORN OIL
- ½ LIME, JUICED

Method:

1. Soak toothpicks in water.
2. Mix 2 teaspoons cumin and 2 teaspoons chili powder in a dish.
3. Preheat an Air Fryer to 400°F.
4. Slice chicken horizontally through the middle and pound.
5. Season chicken with remaining chili powder, remaining cumin, chipotle flakes, oregano, salt, and pepper.
6. Place 1/2 the bell pepper, onion, and jalapeno in the center of 1 breast half.
7. Secure with a toothpick.
8. Roll each one in the chili-cumin mixture in the shallow dish.
9. Drizzle olive oil.
10. Cook chicken for 6 minutes.
11. Top with lime juice and serve.

Main Ingredient: **Chicken**

38_Ranch Chicken Tenders

Total Time:
12 minutes

Serving:
4 persons

Total Carbs:
59 g

Total Calories:
538 kcal

Ingredients:

- 8 CHICKEN TENDERS, RAW
- 1 CUP PANKO BREADCRUMBS
- 1 EGG
- 2 TBSP. WATER
- 1/2 TSP. SALT
- 1/4 TSP BLACK PEPPER
- 1/2 TSP. GARLIC POWDER
- 1/2 TSP. ONION POWDER
- 1/4 TSP. PAPRIKA
- 1 TSP. DRIED PARSLEY

Method:

1. Coat chicken with all the seasonings.

2. Coat chicken with egg wash then with panko.

3. Cook 12 minutes at 400°F flipping midway cooking and serve.

Main Ingredient: **Coconut**

39_Coconut Chicken

Total Time:	**Serving:**	**Total Carbs:**	**Total Calories:**
10 minutes	4 persons	150g	1419 kcal

Ingredients:

- ½ CUP CANNED COCONUT MILK
- ½ CUP PINEAPPLE JUICE
- 2 TBSP. BROWN SUGAR
- 1 TBSP. SOY SAUCE
- 2 TSP. SRIRACHA SAUCE
- 1 TSP. GROUND GINGER
- 1-POUND STRIPED BONELESS SKINLESS CHICKEN BREASTS
- 2 EGGS
- 1 CUP SWEETENED SHREDDED COCONUT
- 1 CUP PANKO BREAD CRUMBS
- 1 ½ TSP. SALT
- ½ TSP. BLACK PEPPER

Method:

1. Coat chicken with coconut milk, pineapple juice, brown sugar, soy sauce, Sriracha sauce, and ginger. Refrigerate.

2. Preheat an Air Fryer to 375°F.

3. Combine shredded coconut, panko, salt, and pepper in a bowl.

4. Dip chicken strips in beaten egg and then in the coconut-panko mixture. Repeat.

5. Cook chicken at 375°F for 6 minutes and turn.

6. Cook for 4 to 6 minutes and serve.

Main Ingredient: **Jalapeno**

40_Jalapeno Popper Stuffed Chicken

Total Time:
20 minutes

Serving:
3 persons

Total Carbs:
27 g

Total Calories:
3038 kcal

Ingredients:

- 12 CHICKEN THIGHS, BONELESS AND SKINLESS
- 6 JALAPENOS
- 125G CREAM CHEESE
- 3 CLOVES GARLIC, MINCED
- 1/2 TSP. ONION POWDER
- 1/2 TSP. CHILI POWDER
- 1/4 TSP. PEPPER
- 1 TSP. SALT
- OIL MIXTURE:
- 4 TBSP. AVOCADO OIL
- 1/4 TSP. CHILI POWDER
- 1/4 TSP. ONION POWDER

Method:

1. Combine the cream cheese, garlic, onion powder, chili powder, salt, and pepper.

2. Cut jalapenos lengthwise and remove the seeds.

3. Add cream cheese to each of the 12 jalapeno halves.

4. Place a jalapeno popper on flattened chicken and roll it up with a toothpick.

5. Brush chicken with oil mixture.

6. Set the temperature to 380°F for 12 minutes.

7. Flip chicken midway cooking and serve.

Main Ingredient: **Pork**

41_Chile Verde Burritos

Total Time:
30 minutes

Serving:
5 persons

Total Carbs:
505 g

Total Calories:
2212 kcal

Ingredients:

- 2 CUPS CHOPPED PULLED PORK
- 1 CUP SALSA VERDE
- 2 TABLESPOONS COTIJA CHEESE
- 10 (6 INCHES) FLOUR TORTILLAS

Method:

1. Mix pulled pork, salsa verde, and cotija cheese in a bowl.
2. Fill tortillas and fold.
3. Air Fry at 400°F for 6 minutes and serve.

Main Ingredient: **Potato**

42_Tacos de Papa

Mexican Cuisine

Total Time:
30 minutes

Serving:
10 persons

Total Carbs:
298 g

Total Calories:
1236 kcal

Ingredients:

- 2 CUPS WATER
- 1 PACKAGE INSTANT MASHED POTATOES
- 1/2 CUP SHREDDED CHEDDAR CHEESE
- 1 GREEN ONION, CHOPPED
- 1/2 TSP. GROUND CUMIN
- 10 CORN TORTILLAS
- 1/2 CUP SALSA VERDE
- 1/4 CUP CRUMBLED COTIJA CHEESE

Method:

1. Make instant mashed potatoes. Stir in cheese, green onion, and cumin.

2. Spread 1 tbsp. potato mixture in the center of tortillas and fold.

3. Cook tacos in batches coated with cooking spray at 400°F for 5 minutes.

4. Drizzle salsa verde over tacos, top with cotija cheese and serve.

Main Ingredient: **Ravioli**

43_Toasted Ravioli Puffs

USA Cuisine

Total Time:
30 minutes

Serving:
6-8 persons

Total Carbs:
31 g

Total Calories:
605 kcal

Ingredients:

- 24 REFRIGERATED CHEESE RAVIOLI
- 1 TBSP. REDUCED-FAT ITALIAN SALAD DRESSING
- 1 TBSP. ITALIAN-STYLE PANKO BREAD CRUMBS
- 1 TBSP. GRATED PARMESAN CHEESE
- 8 TBSP. WARM MARINARA SAUCE

Method:

1. Preheat oven to 400°F.
2. Cook ravioli according to package directions.
3. Brush ravioli with salad dressing.
4. Mix bread crumbs and cheese; sprinkle over ravioli.
5. Bake 12-15 minutes.
6. Serve with marinara sauce.
7.

Main Ingredient: **Tater Tots**

44_Chili Cheese Tater Tots

USA Cuisine

Total Time:
18 minutes

Serving:
4 persons

Total Carbs:
264 g

Total Calories:
2376 kcal

Ingredients:

- 16 OZ. TATER TOTS
- 4 CUPS (3) BEAN CHILI
- 1 CUP WATER
- 1/2 CUP RAW CASHEWS
- HALF VEGETABLE BOUILLON CUBE
- 1/2 TSP. WHITE MISO PASTE
- 2 TBSP. NUTRITIONAL YEAST FLAKES
- 1/4 TSP. CUMIN
- 1/4 TSP. SALT
- 1/4 TSP. ANCHO CHILI POWDER
- 1/4 CUP SLICED GREEN ONIONS

Method:

1. Make tater tots according to package directions.

2. Blend raw cashews, nutritional yeast, white miso paste, water, half of a vegetable bouillon cube, cumin, ancho chili powder, and salt.

3. Cook cashew mixture 10 minutes stirring continuously.

4. Put a layer of tots, 1 cup chili per serving, Queso, and sliced green onions sprinklings and serve.

Main Ingredient: **Turkey**

45_Turkey Breast

Mexican Cuisine

Total Time:
50 minutes

Serving:
6 persons

Total Carbs:
2,5 g

Total Calories:
1720 kcal

Ingredients:

- 1 TBSP. FINELY CHOPPED ROSEMARY
- 1 TSP. FINELY CHOPPED FRESH CHIVES
- 1 TSP. FINELY MINCED GARLIC
- 1/2 TSP. SALT
- 1/4 TSP. BLACK PEPPER
- 2 TBSP. COLD UNSALTED BUTTER
- 2 ¾-POUNDS SKIN-ON, BONE-IN SPLIT TURKEY BREAST

Method:

1. Preheat Air Fryer to 350°F.
2. Mix rosemary, chives, garlic, salt, and pepper with butter until smooth.
3. Coat turkey with butter paste.
4. Air Fry for 20 minutes and turn.
5. Cook for 18 minutes and serve.

Chapter 4

SNACKS

Main Ingredient: **Chicken**

46_Chicken Calzone

Italian Cuisine

Total Time:	**Serving:**	**Total Carbs:**	**Total Calories:**
25 minutes	persons	74 g	497 kcal

Ingredients:

- 1 TSP. OLIVE OIL
- 1/4 CUP CHOPPED RED ONION
- 3-OUNCE BABY SPINACH LEAVES
- 1/3 CUP LOW-SODIUM MARINARA SAUCE
- 2-OUNCE SHREDDED ROTISSERIE CHICKEN BREAST
- 6-OUNCE WHOLE-WHEAT PIZZA DOUGH
- 1 AND A 1/2-OUNCE PRE-SHREDDED PART-SKIM MOZZARELLA CHEESE

Method:

1. Cook onions for 2 minutes at low heat in a skillet.

2. Add spinach and cook for 1 and ½ minutes.

3. Remove pan from heat, and put in marinara sauce and chicken.

4. Put spinach mixture and cheese on a 6-inch dough circle.

5. Fold the dough to form half-moons and seal the edges.

6. Cook in the Air Fryer at 325°F for 12 minutes, turning calzones over after 8 minutes and serve.

Main Ingredient: **Chicken**

47_Chicken Wings

USA Cuisine

Total Time:
30 minutes

Serving:
2 persons

Total Carbs:
30,5 g

Total Calories:
1133 kcal

Ingredients:

- 10 CHICKEN DRUMETTES
- 1 TBSP. LOWER-SODIUM SOY SAUCE
- 1/2 TSP. CORNSTARCH
- 2 TSP. HONEY
- 1 TSP. SAMBAL OELEK
- 1 TSP. FINELY CHOPPED GARLIC
- 1/2 TSP. FINELY CHOPPED FRESH GINGER
- 1 TSP. FRESH LIME JUICE
- 1/8 TSP. KOSHER SALT
- 2 TBSP. CHOPPED SCALLIONS

Method:

1. Air Fry chicken at 400°F for 25 minutes, turning drumettes over midway cooking.

2. Mix soy sauce, cornstarch honey, sambal, garlic, ginger, lime juice, and salt in a small skillet.

3. Thicken mixture on low heat.

4. Coat the chicken with sauce.

5. Sprinkle with scallions and serve.

Main Ingredient: **Corn**

48_Mexican-Style Corn

Mexican Cuisine

Total Time:
18 minutes

Serving:
4 persons

Total Carbs:
150 g

Total Calories:
918 kcal

Ingredients:

- 4 EARS SHUCKED FRESH CORN
- 2 TBSP. CHOPPED FRESH CILANTRO
- 2 TSP. CHOPPED GARLIC
- 1 AND 1/2 TBSP. UNSALTED BUTTER
- 1 TSP. LIME ZEST
- 1/2 TSP. KOSHER SALT
- 1 TBSP. FRESH JUICE
- 1/2 TSP. BLACK PEPPER

Method:

1. Spray corn with cooking spray.

2. Cook corn in the Air Fryer for 14 minutes at 400°F, turning corn over midway through cooking.

3. Mix butter, lime juice, garlic and lime zest in a small microwavable bowl.

4. Microwave for 30 seconds.

5. Put the corn in a dish and put the butter mixture on top.

6. Sprinkle with salt, cilantro and pepper and serve.

Main Ingredient: **Turkey**

49_Chicken and Vegetable Wontons

Chinese Cuisine

Total Time:	**Serving:**	**Total Carbs:**	**Total Calories:**
40 minutes	8-10 persons	1001 g	5594 kcal

Ingredients:

- 1-POUND GROUND TURKEY
- 50 GLUTEN-FREE WONTON WRAPPERS
- 1 TBSP. GINGER, GRATED
- 2 TBSP. SCALLIONS, CHOPPED
- 2 GARLIC CLOVES, MINCED
- 1 TBSP. GLUTEN-FREE SOY SAUCE
- 2 CUPS GREENS SUCH AS BRUSSEL SPROUTS, KALE, AND CABBAGE, CHOPPED
- 2 TBSP. GLUTEN-FREE SWEET CHILI SAUCE
- 1 EGG

Method:

1. Make the wrappers according to the instructions.
2. Slice them into 3-inch squares.
3. Mix ginger, meat, garlic, soy sauce, scallion, greens, and sweet chili sauce.
4. Whisk egg with 1 tbsp. water.
5. Put wonton wrappers on your palm.
6. Brush all 4 edges with egg wash.
7. Put 1 teaspoonful of the stuffing in wrapper wrappers center.
8. Fold wrappers to make wontons.
9. Spray cooking oil on both sides of wontons.
10. Air Fry for 4 minutes at 350°F.
11. Shake Air Fryer basket.
12. Cook for an additional 4 minutes.
13. Serve with extra sweet chili sauce.

Main Ingredient: **Sweet Potato**

50_Sweet Potato Chips

Total Time:	**Serving:**	**Total Carbs:**	**Total Calories:**
30 minutes	1-2 persons	47 g	242 kcal

Ingredients:

- 1 TBSP. COOKING OIL
- 1 SWEET POTATO, UNPEELED, SLICED INTO 1/8-INCH-THICK PIECES
- 1/4 TSP. SEA SALT
- 1 TSP. ROSEMARY, CHOPPED
- 1/4 TSP. BLACK PEPPER

Method:

1. Soak potatoes slices for 20 minutes in cold water.
2. Put oil, salt, and pepper in a bowl.
3. Cook potatoes in batches at 375°F for 25 to 30 minutes.
4. Sprinkle over rosemary and serve.

Conclusion

Air Fryers are a big step towards better health and efficiency. Helping us retain food nutrients and eliminating cooking oil requirement, they ensure us a healthier life.

Air Fryers provide you with all the health and lifestyle benefits without compromising the texture and taste of fried foods. They provide you with the same tasty, crispy brown skin expectations you have from fried foods.

Vortex Air Fryer takes care of you in the tastiest way ever.

THANK YOU

**for choosing my Cookbook
and trying out my delicious
Instant Vortex Air Fryer Recipes!**

Jenny Ellery

CPSIA information can be obtained
at www.ICGtesting.com
Printed in the USA
LVHW072322120521
687092LV00010B/419